1 MONTH OF FREE READING

at

www.ForgottenBooks.com

By purchasing this book you are eligible for one month membership to ForgottenBooks.com, giving you unlimited access to our entire collection of over 1,000,000 titles via our web site and mobile apps.

To claim your free month visit:
www.forgottenbooks.com/free955217

* Offer is valid for 45 days from date of purchase. Terms and conditions apply.

ISBN 978-0-260-54509-1
PIBN 10955217

This book is a reproduction of an important historical work. Forgotten Books uses
state-of-the-art technology to digitally reconstruct the work, preserving the original format
whilst repairing imperfections present in the aged copy. In rare cases, an imperfection in
the original, such as a blemish or missing page, may be replicated in our edition. We do,
however, repair the vast majority of imperfections successfully; any imperfections that
remain are intentionally left to preserve the state of such historical works.

Forgotten Books is a registered trademark of FB &c Ltd.
Copyright © 2018 FB &c Ltd.
FB &c Ltd, Dalton House, 60 Windsor Avenue, London, SW19 2RR.
Company number 08720141. Registered in England and Wales.

For support please visit www.forgottenbooks.com

ANNUAL REPORT

of the

BOARD OF DIRECTORS
and SUPERINTENDENT

of the

CASWELL TRAINING SCHOOL
For Mental Defectives

at

Flag Station, Hines Junction

KINSTON, N. C.

For the Year Ending June 30, 1926

RALEIGH
CAPITAL PRINTING COMPANY
STATE PRINTERS
1926

BOARD OF TRUSTEES

Hon. L. P. Tapp, *Chairman*	Kinston
Hon. L. A. Bethune	Clinton
Dr. W. W. Dawson	Grifton
Dr. G. H. Macon	Warrenton
Mr. S. F. McCotter	Vandemere
Prof. T. E. Whitaker	Oak Ridge
Mr. V. O. Parker	Raleigh
Mr. C. W. Lassiter	Spring Hope
*Mr. J. Harper Alexander	Scotland Neck

EXECUTIVE AND BUILDING COMMITTEE

Hon. L. P. Tapp, *Chairman*	Kinston
Hon. L. A. Bethune	Clinton
Dr. W. W. Dawson	Grifton

*Resigned.

LETTER OF TRANSMITTAL

To His Excellency, Hon. Angus W. McLean,
          Governor of North Carolina.

Dear Sir:—We have the honor of transmitting to your Excellency the Annual Report of the Board of Trustees and Superintendent of The Caswell Training School for mental defectives, for the years 1925 and 1926.

          Respectfully submitted,

                L. P. Tapp, *Chairman,*
                Dr. W. W. Dawson,
                L. A. Bethune,
                      Executive Committee.

OFFICERS OF INSTITUTION

Superintendent:
W. H. DIXON, M.D.

Medical Director:
J. T. WRIGHT, M.D.

Head Nurse:
MISS TEXIE BOWMAN

School Principal:
MISS ELSA ERNST

Head Matron:
MRS. FLORENCE LEONARD

Business Manager:
W. L. SUTTON

SUPERINTENDENT'S REPORT

Mr. Chairman and Members of the Board of Trustees:

I am pleased to make the usual annual report, which is the first report under my administration. I need not note all of the complex conditions existing when I assumed charge. I am pleased to say we do not now have any opposing forces constantly uprising and trying to hinder the success of the institution.

We have secured the services of Dr. J. T. Wright as medical director and psychiatrist. He has proven efficient, willing, and capable for the work of our institution. I also secured Miss Texie Bowman as head nurse. I am pleased with the services she has rendered us. Due to the splendid services of Dr. Wright and Miss Bowman, in my opinion, the health of the institution will compare favorably with any institution with the same kind of inmates and population. (*See reports of Medical Director and Head Nurse.*)

We were unfortunate in losing one of our most efficient attendants, caused by influenza-pneumonia. I refer to Mr. C. M. Morton.

I have tried to improve the personnel of the matrons and attendants, and in a measure I have succeeded. The discipline of the children has improved very much during the past year with the exception of a few. A few, of course, are always a problem.

Dr. James M. Parrott, of Kinston, has been employed as eye, ear, nose, and throat specialist to treat, cure, and correct as many of these troubles as possible. His first work was to make a general examination of every inmate, also noting the condition of the teeth as well as his particular line. During his illness he continued his work by sending his able assistant, Dr. Sabiston.

Another departure was in the securing of Dr. Koonce as dentist, who has been giving two afternoons every week, four hours each, doing extractions, temporary fillings, cleaning, and treatment of pyorrhea. The work of Dr. Wright, Dr. Parrott, and Dr. Koonce will appear in their reports. The report of the school department will explain itself and will follow in the usual order of reports.

COST AND ECONOMY

We had, to begin with, a decrease in the usual appropriation for maintenance for the institution, also found the per capita cost $1.12. By economy in the various departments of the institution and in the meantime getting close coöperation between the different heads of the departments and trying to effect a saving where possible, we have reduced the per capita cost to 84 cents plus per day. The difference between 84 cents and $1.12 is 28 cents, a saving in one day of $108; a saving in 365 days or one year of $39,420. We now have the average cost per day for the institution as a whole $325.16, whereas one year ago it cost $390.06 per day as a whole, when the per capita cost was $1.12.

In practicing economy, we have tried not to let the economy interfere with efficient and proper quantities of food, and in doing this, trying to secure a proper food balance. We have been constantly besieged with calls all over the State for the admission of unfortunate children. This includes calls from morons down to idiots, and after trying to use discretion and good judgment, we have selected those that we could give efficient training that would be a real help to them.

During the early part of the year 1926 work began in the reconstruction of the High Grade Boys' Building. Floors were ordered placed in the Pollock Building, first and second stories. To increase the water supply at our institution, a new pump and reservoir is being installed. We have been constantly handicapped for the lack of water since my administration. It appears now that we will have the use of all these improvements in a very short time.

NEEDS OF THE INSTITUTION IN WAY OF REPAIRS AND IMPROVEMENTS

The cottages are badly in need of repairs, such as plastering and painting, and some other repairs. If it were possible to get them, we should have not less than three more cottages, as I find married help more satisfactory than the single help. I have had, time and again, to refuse married help because of the fact that we did not have the housing facilities for them.

The bathrooms and toilets of the Pollock Building are in such condition that water soaks through these floors. Something, of necessity, must be done to correct this defect.

Your attention has been called to the need of an additional silo at our dairy barn. In my opinion, were this silo erected it would pay for itself in the saving of feed within two years time.

MOVEMENT OF POPULATION

At the beginning of the fiscal year 1925 there were 357 inmates in Caswell Training School. Since then there has been a gradual increase. At the beginning of the fiscal year 1926 we had in our institution 411 inmates. The average number of children was 385 plus. Of this number, 14 have been paroled, 12 died, 27 ran away (20 of these have been returned), 11 were taken home by parents for various causes. Total number of inmates admitted, 89. The vacation months for employes and inmates are July and August. Quite a number of the inmates are now home on vacation and a few of the employes.

TYPES OF TRAINING GIVEN

Training in a generalized way is given according to the mentality of the individual. What training can be given to low-grade imbeciles? Teach them simple commands: how to feed themselves, how to dress themselves, and how to do simple duties in the dormitories, such as bed-making and sweeping. In industrial activities they also may receive some training, such as rug-making and assorting material. In the craft department they are trained to make mats, rugs, and to do other simple work in the training room. For this type of inmate it takes about twenty months to fit him or her to perform one simple task. Some one will ask, "Is it worth the time to train one to do these simple things?" Yes, it gives them something useful to do. Keep them employed, and of course they do not have time to destroy their clothes and the furniture, neither do they have time to engage in mischief-making among themselves; they are much more easily managed and their behavior problems are lessened very much.

We are, at this time, training them to march, and they are very much interested in this. Anything that interests them makes them happy. This is one of the ideals we are trying to reach. When you make one of them happy, you have solved some of their behavior problems.

The mid-grade imbecile, of course, can receive much more training than the low-grade imbecile. From this type, with proper training, we can take care of the majority of work at our institution, such as milking, picking vegetables, preparing vegetables for cooking, and cleaning various utensils and implements about the kitchen. Some are helpers in the dining-room and dormitories. They become very efficient in the art and craft department in weaving, rug-making, flower-making, basketry, tatting, crocheting, and many other things too numerous to mention.

The moron or high-grade type can be taught to do vocational and industrial work that the normal can do. There is no limit to their training if you are careful to direct them in what they are interested. The higher and more responsible duties are done largely by this type. Among these duties are: laundering, sewing, house-cleaning, dairying, and farming, which includes plowing, mowing, wagon-driving, hay-making, harvesting corn and other grain. We expect, in the near future, to begin training in painting, carpentry, shoe repairing, gardening, and the taking care of grounds around the buildings.

We try to make them as efficient as possible through the various lines of training. When it becomes possible for inmates to be paroled or discharged from the institution, they will be more or less self-supporting; but, of course, they will always have to be supervised at all times.

This is a brief outline of the training of the Caswell Training School. Any academic schooling here is given only so far as it will fit inmates to be trained in the various activities of the institution.

For the information of the Directors, I wish to say that those employes that have been with the institution one year get two weeks leave of absence with pay; those less than one year, one week with pay.

I wish to thank the Board of Directors for the splendid coöperation and helpful advice given to me during my administration. I am further pleased to know there has not been the least friction or discord in any of the meetings and discussions, and gladly say that you have lived up to the promises made me the day I accepted the Superintendency of Caswell Training School.

W. H. DIXON, M.D.,
Superintendent.

HOSPITAL REPORT
From September 1, 1925, to July 1, 1926
BY
Texie L. Bowman, *Head Nurse*

For the past ten months I have been acting as Head Nurse to the institution, and by the help and encouragement of our Superintendent and Medical Director, things have been going along very nicely in the hospital.

I have had competent nurses most of the time, and I want to extend my appreciation to Dr. Dixon and Dr. Wright for the consideration and courtesy they have shown me during the past ten months. As near as possible, I have kept an accurate daily report of the hospital cases, diagnoses, admissions, discharges, etc. The morning clinic, which is held for the benefit of the children of the institution, has decreased about one-half since September, 1925.

Number of Children Admitted to the Hospital During the Past Ten Months

Month	Count	Month	Count
September	60	February	127
October	60	March	116
November	52	April	86
December	18	May	68
January	50	June	50

Diagnosis of Hospital Cases

Diagnosis	Count	Diagnosis	Count
Hydrocephalus	2	Syphilis	8
Epilepsy	30	Menorrhagia	10
Old sores	18	Colds	40
Sprains	6	Scabies	38
Nervous diseases	9	Abrasions	1
Croup	20	Arthritis, acute	2
Rhus-Toxicodendron	35	Rhinitis, acute	2
Female trouble	6	Diarrhea	30
Wounds infected	2	Erysipelas	2
Bronchitis	16	Stomatitis	8
Idiots	14	Hordeolum	6
Stomach disturbance	25	Dysmenorrhea	10
Pyorrhea	16	Eczema	8
Wounds lacerated	1	Chicken-pox	10
Endocarditis, chronic	1	Pregnancy	1
Broncho-pneumonia	10	Otitis media	1
Tonsillitis	42	Burns, first and second degree	10
Influenza-pneumonia	18	Ulcers	6
Fractures	1	Abscesses	6
Gastro-enteritis	8	Gonorrhea	4
Cystitis, acute, chronic	10	Furuncles	4

Number of Deaths and Causes

Dorothy Adams—Broncho-pneumonia
Roger Burgess—Tuberculosis.
Hallett Spencer—Acute dilatation of the heart.
Lizzie Thaxton—Rheumatoid arthritis.
Pauline Beatty—Acute dilatation of the heart.
George Boyles—Broncho-pneumonia.
Catherine Rogers—Broncho-pneumonia.
Hattie Mae Holland—Inanition induced by gastritis.
Willie Allen—Broncho-pneumonia.
Ethel Clarke—Broncho-pneumonia.
Mittie Shore's unnamed boy—Still-born.

Children Treated at the Dispensary

Tonsillitis	44	Furuncles	45
Stomatitis	55	Wounds lacerated	5
Ulcers	15	Wounds infected	17
Abscesses	32	Otitis media	1
Sprains	8	Pyorrhea	40
Burns (radiator)	6	Cuts	18
Gonorrhea	10		

Number of urinalyses 52
Number of miscroscopic examinations 20
Number of Wassermann examinations 15
Number of physical examinations:
  Adults 20
  Children 140

  Total 160

WORK DONE IN DENTAL DEPARTMENT
From March 12, 1926, to June 1, 1926
By Dr. E. T. Koonce, *Dentist*

Cement filling 17
Amalgam filling 276
Porcelain filling 46
Extractions 54
Treatments 27
Gums treated 8
Scaling and polishing 89

WORK DONE AT EYE, EAR, NOSE, AND THROAT CLINIC
From August 1, 1925, to June 1, 1926

Dr. Parrott made examinations of all the children in the institution during the months of August, September, October, and November. Dr. Sabiston came one day in every week during the months of December, January, February, March, April, May, and June.

Examinations made in December 48
Examinations made in January 32
Examinations made in February 30
Examinations made in March 28

Examinations made in April.. 32
Examinations made in May.. 40
Examinations made in June... 38
Total number of Neo-Salvarsan treatments............................ 8
Mixed treatment by mouth... 15
Number of children taking Pituitary 18
Number of children taking Thyroid 41
Number of children taking Luminal 24

Number of epileptic attacks during the months—
  September.. 152
  October.. 180
  November... 201
  December... 177
  January.. 150
  February.. 120
  March... 90
  April... 106
  May.. 130
  June.. 165

Respectfully submitted,

TEXIE L. BOWMAN,
Head Nurse.

WORK OF SEWING DEPARTMENT
From June 30, 1925, to June 30, 1926

Rompers	502
Shirts	475
Dresses	638
Overalls	456
Bloomers	89
Aprons	202
Slips	327
Gowns	401
Drawers	82
Drawers and bodies	281
Pants	39
Tablecloths	4
Blouses	172
Teddies	174
Brassiers	146
Sheets	181
Infants' shirts	5
Coats	29
Union suits	54
Night shirts	74
Napkins	90
Pillow-slips	6

PRODUCTS RECEIVED FROM THE FARM

Green peas, shelled (lbs.)	1,277
Syrup (gals.)	550
Cabbage (lbs.)	11,227
Squash (lbs.)	7,949
String beans (lbs.)	2,392
Cucumbers (lbs.)	8,585
Beets (lbs.)	5,981
Lettuce (lbs.)	486
Tomatoes	30,109
Watermelons	3,533
Cantaloupes	4,970
Ears corn	12,975
Dry peas (lbs.)	113
Turnips (lbs.)	6,652
Sweet potatoes (bus.)	2,244
Peanuts (bus.)	61
Collards (lbs.)	12,950
Rutabagas (lbs.)	639
Kale salad (lbs.)	2,141
Onions (lbs.)	1,302
Spinach (lbs.)	94
Strawberries (qts.)	1,517
Garden peas, shelled (lbs.)	817
Dewberries (qts.)	5,463
White potatoes (bus.)	962
Meat (lbs.)	14,639
Eggs (doz.)	1,658
Chickens, dressed (lbs.)	343
Broilers (lbs.)	935
Milk (gals.)	35,242
Beef (lbs.)	2,395
Goat (lbs.)	1,200

ITEMIZED STATEMENT EXPENDITURES—MAINTENANCE FUND

From June 30, 1925, to June 30, 1926

Maintenance appropriation, 1925-1926..$118,750.00
Receipts for 1925-1926...3,973.66

   Total maintenance appropriation...$122,723.66

EXPENDITURES

OFFICE AND ADMINISTRATION.

1101	Executive salaries	$ 7,060.89
1103	Clerical salaries	1,778.33
1104	Inspectional salaries	511.50
1109	Per diem and fees	894.42
1201	Office supplies	148.25
1301	Postage	303.14
1302	Telephone and telegraph	331.96
1303	Freight, express, and drayage	25.20
1401	Hotel and meals	
1402	Railroad and other fares	337.50
1403	Mileage allowance	36.60
1501	Printing, stationery, office forms, etc.	248.68
1508	Publication of notices and advertising	114.58
1601	Motor vehicles upkeep	2,360.59
1902	Rent of buildings, offices, and lands	275.50
1903	Rent of equipment	4.50
1905	Miscellaneous expense	75.22
2203	Premiums on official bonds	20.00
3101	Office equipment and furnishings	66.21
3107	Motor vehicles purchased	1,436.75
1210	Library supplies	44.00

   Total..$ 16,073.82

SUBSISTENCE.

1105	Supervisors' salaries	$ 2,052.62
1106	Skilled labor	2,630.53
1107	Unskilled labor	36.56
3103	Dining-room and kitchen equipment	724.32
1216	Shop supplies and materials	30.23
1203A	Meats, fish, and fowl	2,984.46
1203B	Dairy products and eggs	62.56
1203C	Cereal food products	6,792.92
1203D	Vegetables	1,602.01
1203E	Fruits and nuts	824.73
1203F	Saccharine products	1,882.23
1203G	Beverages	575.19
1203H	Condiments, flavors, and pickles	245.62
1203I	Fats, oils, and miscellaneous provisions	1,122.20

   Total..21,566.18

HOUSEKEEPING.

1105	Supervisors' salaries	$ 1,630.00	
1202	Cleaning and household supplies	1,607.93	
1204	Sewing supplies and dry goods	2,148.95	
1217	Ice and other refrigeration supplies	1,756.40	
1222	Wearing apparel purchased	1,271.57	
1223	Miscellaneous fuel	18.90	
1216	Shop supplies and materials	154.44	
3102	Institutional furniture and furnishings	1,351.10	
3104	Bedding and linens	1,021.36	
3119	Plumbing equipment	58.50	
3120	Electrical equipment	362.13	
1106	Skilled labor	1,173.33	
	Total		$ 12,554.61

LAUNDERING.

1105	Supervisors' salaries	$ 1,072.19	
1205	Laundry supplies	703.79	
1904	Outside laundering and cleaning	77.00	
3105	Laundry equipment	179.25	
	Total		2,032.23

MEDICAL AND SURGICAL CARE.

1102	Professional and technical salaries	$ 2,263.51	
1206	Medical and surgical supplies	380.95	
1207	Drugs and medicines	1,215.73	
1208	Laboratory supplies and materials	64.60	
3106	Medical and surgical equipment	30.08	
	Total		3,954.87

NURSING AND ATTENDANCE.

1102	Professional and technical salaries	$ 105.00	
1105	Supervisors' salaries	1,104.09	
1107	Unskilled labor	9,770.87	
	Total		10,979.96

LIGHT, HEAT, POWER, AND WATER.

1106	Skilled labor	$ 1,496.93	
1107	Unskilled labor	1,875.00	
1108	Cummutation	26.00	
1218	Power and heating plant supplies	474.98	
1224	Coal (including freight)	13,049.61	
1701	Light, power, and water	550.47	
3118	Power and heating plant equipment	1,548.40	
	Total		19,021.39

CARE OF BUILDINGS, GROUNDS, AND EQUIPMENT.

1106	Skilled labor	$ 2,208.33
1107	Unskilled labor	82.70
1213	Botanical and grounds supplies	492.01
1219	Plumbing supplies and materials	280.59
1220	Electrical supplies and materials	123.71
1221	General supplies and materials	2,001.38
1802	Repairs to building and structures	70.37
3121	General equipment	191.62
3116	Shop equipment	42.75

Total .... $ 5,493.46

INSTRUCTIONAL.

1204	Sewing supplies and dry goods	$ 2.00
1209	Classroom and teachers' supplies	257.79
1102	Professional and technical salaries	4,326.20
3109	Classroom and teachers' equipment	18.81

Total 4,604.80

AGRICULTURAL.

1105	Supervisors' salaries	$ 2,616.60
1107	Unskilled labor	4,452.37
1214	Farm and dairy supplies	5,021.47
1215	Forage and supplies for animals	9,580.54
3114	Farm and dairy equipment	245.55
3115	Livestock	485.00

Total 22,401.53

$118,682.85

Maintenance appropriation $122,723.66
Expenditures 118,682.85

Unexpended balance of appropriation, June 30, 1926 .... $ 4,040.81

REPORT OF EDUCATIONAL DEPARTMENT

The activities of the educational department during the past year included:

1. Departmental reorganization.
2. Completion and classification of pupils throughout the institution.
3. Academic and general training classes.
4. Household classes and training for domestic service.
5. Manual training and craft work.
6. Night classes in citizenship training.
7. Physical education, general school exercises, and recreational activities.
8. Industrial training in institutional work assignments.
9. Teacher training and supervision.
10. Testing and educational research problems.

There are certain points in regard to the training of pupils in a school for feebleminded that may be fitly emphasized:

Feeblemindedness is a condition, *not* a disease; hence a training school is *not* a hospital—its function is not primarily therapeutic, but *educational*.

We do not "cure" children—we *train* them.

Training cannot *give* a child intelligence; it can only aid him in the development and efficient direction of that intelligence (be it little or much) with which nature has endowed him.

If we can train a higher grade child to launder, sew, read, write, work in the dairy or on the farm, it is because he has the innate ability to learn these things and profit by them, not because we have increased his intelligence.

To develop in the right direction a child's emotions and powers of will or self-control is as important as to train his intelligence.

It is the function of the educational department to study the individual needs of every pupil, and so to group these pupils that we may train them, not necessarily to the limit of their academic possibilities, but to the limit of what they can *use effectively*—both of handwork and headwork—in everyday life, for their own welfare and that of others.

It is also the function of this department, by making available its experience, to aid in the right care and training of those feebleminded outside the institution who can profit best by extra-institutional care.

Finally, the whole problem of the education of the feebleminded is today a specialized field. It demands patience, wisdom, *special training,* and, above all, a sense of relative values.

1. DEPARTMENTAL REORGANIZATION.

Beginning with September, 1925, the previous educational and craft departments were reorganized as one department, cutting the overhead expenses for the combined departments to half the cost of the previous year.

2. CLASSIFICATION.

Figure I shows the total number of inmates (411) grouped according to their wards and buildings. The number of pupils of each degree of mental deficiency is shown for every ward, and for the institution as a whole. It must be borne in mind, however, that there is no sharp dividing line between the various grades of mental deficiency, any more than between mental defect and normality. Each group merges gradually into the next. The object of the chart is to permit a rapid survey of the general classification within the institution.

Figure II shows the percentage of low-grade and higher grade pupils usually found in institutions for feebleminded, as compared with the percentage of low and higher grades at present in The Caswell Training School. The percentage and number of pupils in each training group at Caswell are also shown. It will be seen that so large a percentage of lower grade pupils form a serious handicap to the progress of the higher grade pupils in the institution.

The classification of pupils throughout the institution, in connection with the educational work during the past year, was as follows:

The academic and general training classes that formed the nucleus of the school department during 1925-26 included the 75 children in the institution who were from 3-10 years mentally, and under 16 years of age. One pupil over 16 was taken into these classes from special training during the second school term. This boy, with an I.Q. of 61, had had very little previous schooling, and progressed from I to III grade standard in the minimum essentials of reading, writing, and practical arithmetic in four months time, in addition to his work in other classes (manual training, etc.).

The pupils in the household training or home economics classes ranged in age from 13 years upwards, and from 6-12 years in mentality.

The junior manual training classes (one girls' group and one boys' group.) ranged in age from 9-16 years, and from 5-10 years in mentality. The girls' senior craft classes included 64 pupils over 16 years of age, and from 4-12 years mentally.

A small group of farm boys, ranging in age from 17-24 years, and from 6-12 years in mentality, voluntarily attended night classes twice a week in the school department. The above classes included 156 pupils in all.

Further industrial training of pupils was undertaken in the various institutional work assignments. The majority of these pupils were

The Caswell Training School

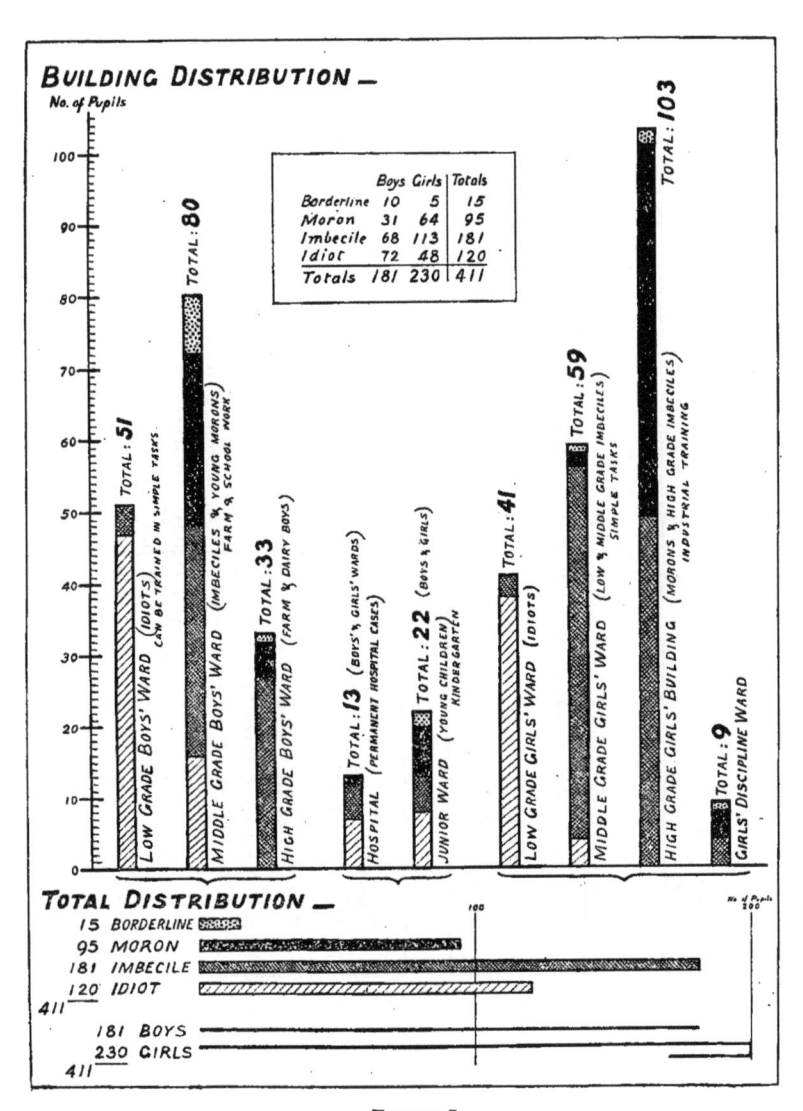

BUILDING DISTRIBUTION —

	Boys	Girls	Totals
Borderline	10	5	15
Moron	31	64	95
Imbecile	68	113	181
Idiot	72	48	120
Totals	181	230	411

- TOTAL: 51 — LOW GRADE BOYS' WARD (IDIOTS) CAN BE TRAINED IN SIMPLE TASKS
- TOTAL: 80 — MIDDLE GRADE BOYS' WARD (IMBECILES & YOUNG MORONS) FARM & SCHOOL WORK
- TOTAL: 33 — HIGH GRADE BOYS' WARD (FARM & DAIRY BOYS)
- TOTAL: 13 — HOSPITAL (BOYS' & GIRLS' WARDS) (PERMANENT HOSPITAL CASES)
- TOTAL: 22 — JUNIOR WARD (BOYS & GIRLS) (YOUNG CHILDREN KINDERGARTEN)
- TOTAL: 41 — LOW GRADE GIRLS' WARD (IDIOTS)
- TOTAL: 59 — MIDDLE GRADE GIRLS' WARD (LOW & MIDDLE GRADE IMBECILES) SIMPLE TASKS
- TOTAL: 103 — HIGH GRADE GIRLS' BUILDING (MORONS & HIGH GRADE IMBECILES) INDUSTRIAL TRAINING
- TOTAL: 9 — GIRLS' DISCIPLINE WARD

TOTAL DISTRIBUTION —

- 15 BORDERLINE
- 95 MORON
- 181 IMBECILE
- 120 IDIOT
- 411

- 181 BOYS
- 230 GIRLS
- 411

FIGURE I

Showing the status of the population at The Caswell Training School on July 1, 1926. (For differentiation between high and low grade imbeciles, see Figure II.)

FIGURE II

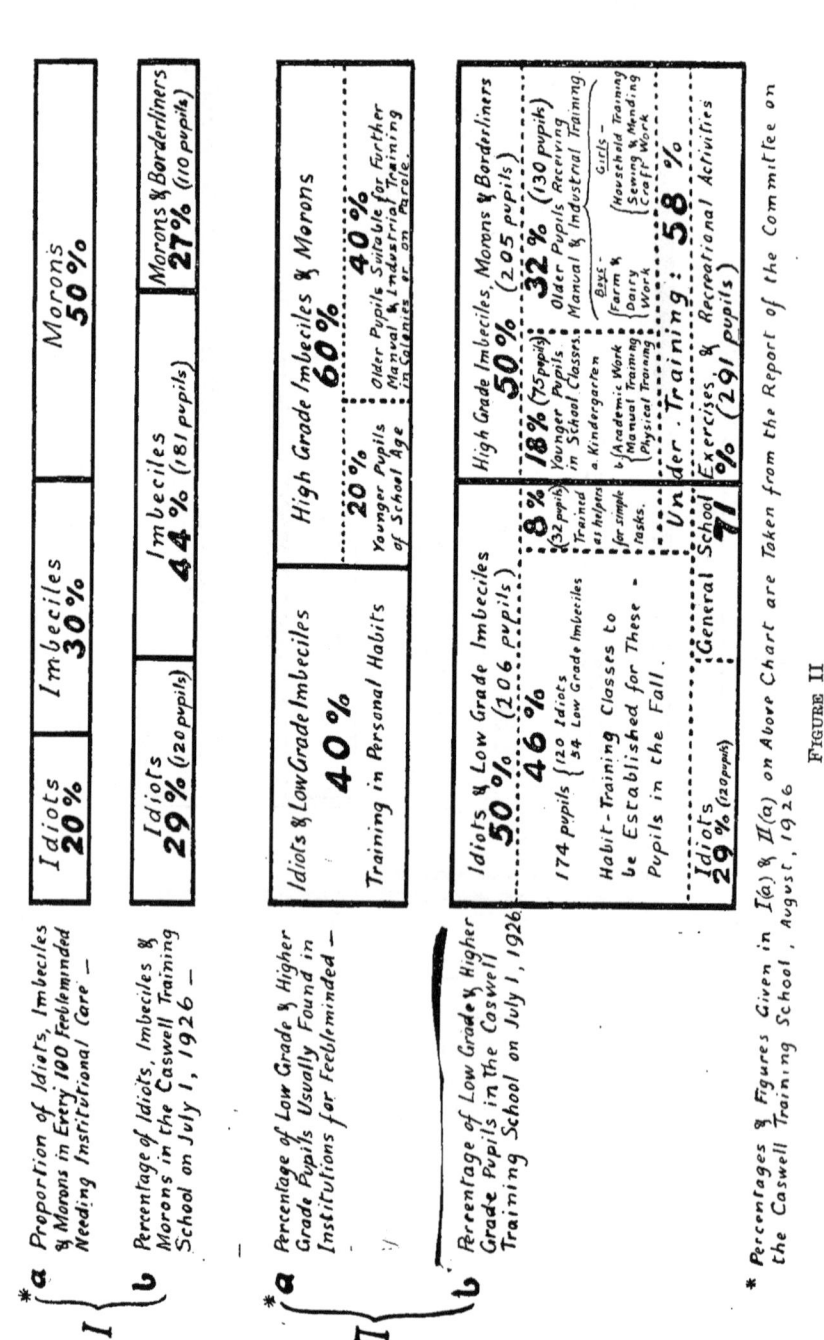

Showing the handicap under which The Caswell Training School labors, due to the preponderance of low-grade material over 16 years of age, with a mental age range from 5-12 years. In addition, 32 lower grade imbeciles were employed in simple tasks around the institution and as helpers in the wards. This brought the number of pupils under training up to 237.

All pupils of imbecile and moron level attended chapel exercises three times a week, and for special exercises on holiday occasions. In connection with the recreational activities of the institution, pupils were classified also into socially homogeneous groups.

The school department thus concerned itself more or less directly with every one of the 291 pupils within the institution who are above the idiot level. For the latter (i.e., the idiots) we hope to establish habit-training classes in the fall, such as are found in all up-to-date institutions of our type elsewhere.

3. ACADEMIC AND GENERAL TRAINING CLASSES.

The academic and general training classes (*"Practice Classes,"* as we prefer to call them) for pupils under 16 consisted of five classes, i.e., three groups of young and lower grade pupils at pre-kindergarten and kindergarten level, and two "Advanced Groups" of higher grade pupils —one for the boys and one for the girls.

The aim in the three lower groups was to establish, by means of physical training, sense training and the kindergarten gifts and occupations, and a groundwork of correct habits on which to build later practical household, manual, academic, and industrial training as suited to the intelligence of the pupils.

The academic work in the boys' and girls' "Advanced Groups" included in its program a certain minimum amount of graded work in reading, writing, and arithmetic, from I to IV grade standard. In general, a pupil was expected to reach the grade standard *indicated by his mental age.*

From one hour to an hour and a half out of the school day was spent on this work, the remainder of the pupils' school time being spent on manual, physical, and industrial training. This gives a fair idea of the relative importance attached to academic training in the institution. It is by no means considered the only type of training necessary. It covers only from one-fifth to one-fourth of the higher grade pupils' school day. For the boys and girls in these "Advanced Groups" reading, writing, and some practical arithmetic form at least a necessary *part* of their future working equipment. They are sufficiently intelligent to profit by such instruction, and are being trained to become future wage-earners in colonies or on parole. For them, therefore, with double significance education is "a *habit-training program,* a matter of *getting the right habits."*

All the school classes meet in the chapel every morning for "Morning Exercises" before going to their classrooms. These exercises are opened regularly with the flag salute and the National Anthem. Wherever possible, the classes have been encouraged to help each other and work together for the good of the entire group. In all classes, the importance of forming the right working habits—habits of obedience, exactness, cheerfulness, trustworthiness, "stick-to-itiveness," and *thrift*—was constantly stressed by providing the children with the right kind of opportunity for establishing such habits. As an example of "working together" and lessons of "thrift," the following might be cited: The furniture used for the past year and a half in the pre-kindergarten class was old, discarded kitchen furniture which was painted and made over by the boys' manual training class. It serves its present purpose admirably. In the same class, too, most of the teaching material (including 300 blocks made by the boys) was fashioned out of waste material.

The floor of the "gym" was also repaired by the boys.

4. HOUSEHOLD CLASSES AND TRAINING FOR DOMESTIC SERVICE.

The domestic science classes undertook simple household cookery and care of the home. The afternoon classes in practical housekeeping assumed the general care of the schoolrooms and chapel, while the morning housekeeping classes undertook to care for a small group of bedrooms and living-room. This provided household training of the most practical kind. The work was carefully graded, each child being kept at an allotted task until that task was thoroughly learned, before being given a more difficult task. Daily records of the work was kept by the teacher in charge of the classes. As a result of this training we are now able to place these pupils directly to more responsible tasks in the general work of the institution, while others who have since been paroled to their own homes will find there the opportunity to make practical use of their training.

5. MANUAL TRAINING AND CRAFT WORK.

a. Boys' Junior Manual Training Class.

The work in this class included simple woodwork projects, involving the correct use of saw, plane, and hammer, and the finishing of surfaces (sandpapering, painting, varnishing, etc.). The completed projects included a book cupboard, set of shelves, coat hangers, additional blocks and toys for the younger children, a number of odd mending jobs in the school department (table, drawers, cupboard, etc.), and the staging used for the various school exercises throughout the year. Some of the work done in this class during the previous year has already been mentioned.

The stenciling done by the boys during the past year and a half included a club banner and badges, commercial lettering for practical purposes around the institution, a large stenciled curtain, and other articles for institutional use. Some block printing and poster work was done towards the end of this year.

b. Girls' Junior Manual Training Class.

This class did some plain sewing and simple craft work; also poster work and various other types of hand work more or less closely correlated with the academic class work. The aim in this class was to give the initial training on which to build later more advanced manual and industrial training in the senior craft classes and institutional work assignments.

c. Girls' Senior Craft Classes.

These three senior classes made over 550 articles during the year, including 44 rugs woven on the looms. About half of these rugs were made out of waste material, the strips for the rugs being torn, cut and sewed by lower grade pupils.

Some of the articles made in the craft room were placed in use in the institution, some were used as additional Christmas gifts for the pupils, and others were sold to supply further material for craft work. Two exhibits were prepared during the year, one being sent to the Franklin County Fair, Louisburg, and the other to the Welfare Workers' Conference, Greensboro. The decorations and costumes for the various exercises and entertainments given by the children were also made in the craft room.

While the amount of work turned out by these classes was considerable, we were not primarily concerned with the output, but rather with the training value of the work for the pupils. All of the work was taught in carefully graded steps, and each project subdivided into "jobs" requiring different grades of ability. In this way many tasks became "community projects" at which different pupils, varying widely in intellectual endowment, worked harmoniously together towards some common end.

6. NIGHT CLASSES IN CITIZENSHIP TRAINING.

The term "citizenship training" is here used to denote only the simplest and most elementary type of training for community living. Complexity of environment and citizenship activities vary widely in any community, but democracy demands that even the humblest individual develop certain habits and attitudes that are primarily assential to community well-being and progress. The stable higher grade boy in the institution, who is working steadily day by day, and looking forward to parole, needs some such additional training. Here in later adolescence ideas may be got across and the boy develop a social maturity (within limits) that lay beyond his grasp at an earlier age.

All the boys who voluntarily attended these night classes were above the age limit of the regular school classes (i.e., over 16 years), and worked full time on the farm in the daytime. Their school achievements ranged from I to V grade. The main problem was to give them what they ought to have along with that they wanted. All wanted to take further work in reading. So by using for the less advanced pupils such books as "The Country Life Reader" (an adult beginners' reader) and for the more advanced pupils the daily papers and suitable books and magazines,. a wide range of topics was brought up for discussion. Such points as saving, the care of one's own and other people's property, how to keep a bank account, "safety first" programs, fire prevention, forest conservation, etc., aroused a keen interest when linked up with the boys' daily activities and their future outside the institution.

We realize that mere discussions and the forming of opinions mean little unless carried over into action and concrete habit-training; also that physical training and further training for constructive use of leisure time should be included in even the simplest program of citizenship training. It will be evident, therefore, that the work done in these night classes was more or less in the nature of a "try-out"—a mere beginning. We hope, with the opening of our new boys' building this fall, to develop this phase of the work further.

7. PHYSICAL EDUCATION, GENERAL SCHOOL EXERCISES, AND RECREATIONAL ACTIVITIES.

a. Physical Education.

The aim of the work in physical education is fourfold: (1) Training for muscular coördination; (2) Health maintenance; (3) Citizenship training (development of "team spirit" and ideas of fair play); (4) Recreation.

Beyond the elementary work done in the kindergarten classes, the physical training classes during the past year included two groups, the junior boys' group and the junior girls' group. These corresponded to the boys' and girls' advanced school groups, and junior manual training classes.

The junior boys' physical training class and scout work were directed by Mr. Morton, in addition to his building work, until the latter part of the year, when the passing away of this fine worker and friend of the boys left us without anyone to carry on the regular class in gymnastics, military tactics (marching, facing, wheeling, etc.), track work and field games. The scout work was given into Mrs. Morton's charge, at her request, and the work of preparation for the tenderfoot examination carried forward to the end of the school year. We are anxious to have this work established as a regular part of the recreational activities on the boys' side, and appreciate the interest shown by Scout Executive W. W. Rivers, of Goldsboro, and a number of Kinston friends. The boys' eagerness to continue the work speaks for itself.

The program in the junior girls' physical training class covered the various activities enumerated in the "North Carolina Syllabus in Physical Education, for Elementary Grades," up to III grade difficulty.

The work thus included health habit training, correct posture work, gymnastic lessons, marching, facing and wheeling, plays and games, rhythmic exercises and athletic contests. Marked progress was made by this group.

The work in physical education is much hampered by lack of proper facilities. The "gym" (an old kitchen with the partitions taken out) needs lining and heating for winter work. Two dozen pairs of dumb-bells bought this year represent our sole equipment. Additional equipment and provision for physical training of older pupils is needed.

b. General School Exercises.

The chapel exercises which were held three times a week throughout the school year, for all pupils above the idiot level, included (a) Wednesday morning exercises at which stories and simple patriotic and seasonal instruction were interspersed with school songs and individual and group items by pupils; (b) Friday night moving-picture shows; (c) Sunday afternoon religious exercises. The Wednesday and Sunday exercises opened regularly with the flag salute by the entire assembly, and the national anthem or some other patriotic song.

Special entertainments were held to celebrate Hallowe'en, Armistice Day, Thanksgiving, Christmas, Washington's Birthday, and Easter. In addition, two successful concerts were given outside the institution, at Kinston and Ayden, and elicited favorable press comment. Our thanks are due to the management of the Kinston Grand Theatre and the president of the Ayden Seminary for their kindly coöperation and the use of their buildings for our performances.

The programs in these eight different entertainments throughout the year were rendered entirely by the pupils, and consisted of plays, recitations, rhythmic exercises, and vocal and pianoforte items. The work was produced mainly under the tuition of the music teacher, with the assistance of other members of the teaching staff. The pupils' choir, quartet, and singing classes contributed largely to the success of the programs, as did also the dainty costumes and stage decorations made by the craft classes.

The pianoforte work covered by a few specially chosen pupils who could profit by it and thus render, when needed, useful service in playing for the marching and other work of classes, has given gratifying results. Two pupils in particular show special music ability beyond the general level of their intelligence (high grade moron). During the past year, in addition to their other class work, they have made musical progress equal to that of the average normal child. Their work has contributed much to the various exercises of the institution, and to the happiness of the children in general.

Program work, we find, does much to clinch and illumine, from the child's point of view, the work done in other classes. It gives, also, that invaluable thing to children who have hitherto looked upon themselves as failures—a feeling of success, and public approbation. Last, but not least, it adds considerably to the happiness of the pupils—both performers and audience.

c. Recreational Activities.

The annual visit to the Kinston Fair of around three hundred of our pupils is one of the most eagerly anticipated events in our children's lives, and the kindness of the management in allowing our children free entrance to the grounds, and to the various shows and amusements, is much appreciated.

The Christmas packages sent to our children by the Philathea classes from all over North Carolina is another annual source of joy to the pupils. The packages are sent to those pupils (150 pupils) who have no "home folks" to remember them at Christmas time. These gifts bespeak the loving care and thoughtfulness of those who make Christmas an occasion for remembering others less fortunate than themselves.

We are also indebted to the following for the happy events that were occasioned by their thoughtfulness: to the management of the Grand Theatre, Kinston, for allowing our pupils free entrance to performances at the theatre during Thanksgiving week, and to the State College Band, Ayden Seminary Glee Club, and the Oxford Orphanage, for the delightful entertainments they gave to our children.

Of the further recreational activities directed within the institution may be mentioned numberless hikes after work hours, on Saturday afternoons, Sundays, and special holidays. There were also occasional weiner roasts, and during the winter a series of simple little parties, consisting of an hour's indoor games with pieces of candy as prizes. These outings and parties included the different groups of pupils in the various school classes and work details.

8. Industrial Training in Institutional Work Assignments.

a. Schedule of Assignments.

Many of our pupils have remained for years in one or two departments. This did not make it possible to consider the needs of either the children or the institution in regard to the more varied industrial training of pupils. The parole of a number of older pupils and the influx of new untrained ones left several work details considerably understaffed in the way of trained workers. It was necessary, therefore, to provide for some more comprehensive and adequate scheme of training than had existed heretofore. The aim of the present schedule of assignments is to assist in providing a thorough and practical training for possible parole candidates, and also to insure an adequate, continuous supply of trained institution workers for the various details.

Before planning the schedule, ratings for each pupil in quality of work and behavior were obtained from those in charge of each of the departments in which a child had worked. A five-point rating scale was used. These ratings, together with the mental age of a pupil, his "achievement quotient," special aptitudes (where such existed) and peculiarities of temperament, as well as the most suitable type of training for each individual pupil at present, were all duly considered in the placing of every child in the schedule. Special effort was made to arrange suitable programs for problem pupils.

b. Training and Progress.

A daily record of the pupils' progress in each department was kept. In this way we have been able to keep check on the progress of every pupil, and much worth-while training has been accomplished by the matrons and those in charge. Some buildings maintained a very high standard of household training for their pupils—notably, the discipline ward and the hospital. In the junior ward one higher grade girl was trained as kindergarten helper by the matron in charge, who directed a kindergarten class for the small children in addition to her other work on the ward. Much has been done to raise the pupils' standard of work in the various work departments. For example, in the sewing room the garments are better made, and here as elsewhere the children took pride in producing a superior article, and increasing their speed of work at the same time. The value of such training for the future wage-earning capacity of the pupils, as well as for institutional efficiency, is obvious.

In regard to the training of children of lower mentality, one girl with a five-year mind has learned, in carefully graded steps, first to sew on buttons, next the cutting and sewing of strips for rag carpets, and now she has started making quilts. She has also made a fair attempt at buttonholes. In the mending room a number of high-grade imbeciles have learned to patch and mend very nicely. We hope to extend this work downwards, and with the further development of our seguin or pre-kindergarten classes, we expect to train all our low-grade and mid-grade imbeciles to do many types of useful, simple routine work under supervision. The building matron in charge of these children during the past few months has given much time and thought to training them in habits of obedience and personal cleanliness, and will assist in their additional training during the coming year.

9. TEACHER TRAINING AND SUPERVISION.

A definite program in teacher training and supervision was carried on throughout the year. A schedule of three lecture hours per week, in general classroom management, educational psychology, and psychology and pedagogy of the subnormal, for a period of 30 weeks, made a total of 100 hours of class work, including 10 hours of demonstration in addition to 90 lecture hours. Upon recommendation from the Department of Psychology at the University of North Carolina, one of its graduate students who intends to take up Special Class work in the public schools of North Carolina this fall, attended the teacher training classes at The Caswell Training School for the month of June, giving at the same time her teaching services to the school.

10. TESTING AND EDUCATIONAL RESEARCH PROBLEMS.

Psychometric examinations (Terman) made during the period from June 1, 1925, to July 1, 1926, were as follows:

Clinic cases	14
Institution cases	41
	55

A series of charts for administrative use in a school for feebleminded and in Special Class work is being developed. The purpose of these charts will be to indicate the relations between chronological age, mental age, intelligence quotient, school placement, and probable educational and occupational programs. In this way we hope to make it possible that such information in regard to any particular pupil or group of pupils can be readily arranged in a convenient graphic form for the use of teachers and administrators. The charts are a modification of the "Providence Personnel Charts" worked out by Dr. Richard D. Allen, lecturer in vocational guidance at Harvard University and director of research and guidance in the public schools of Providence, R. I. The "Institutional Personnel Chart" and the "Special Class Chart" are based on the study of 1,200 institutional and Special Class pupils, including 425 present and past pupils of The Caswell Training School.

E. ERNST, *Principal.*